Going D1

When Skills & Talent *ain't* enough

Stanley "Stack" Williams Jr., MBA

ISBN: 1987768248
ISBN-13: 9781987768244

Dedication

I' am blessed and beyond grateful for my beloved mother. Mommy, I know it was very challenging for you to raise me as a single mom in the inner city, but you did it. You have done and continue to do so much for me. I' am honored to call you my mother. I decided to dedicate this book to you because you represent the reality of many single parent households headed by mothers. I know first-hand the struggles that we endured as a result of not having an athletic advocate or someone to truly invest in the nurturing of my own ability. Again, thank you mommy, I love you…"Lil Stash"

PLAYBOOK

Team Prayer

- Thank you to Miss Janet Davenport aka "Aunty", for believing in me and giving me a chance. I am truly appreciative for you aunty.

- Thank you to everyone that volunteered their time in editing this book. Shawndel, Tot, Mario, Tim, and Endia. You guys provided excellent feedback and I' am grateful for that. Glen, thank you for your clutch advice and consistent support with this project at the last minute bro. You are amazing! Kristen they say the little things matter most, I want to thank you for your early support in this project as you were the plug for my EPK which proved to be vital in writing this project. Salute to you Queen.

- To the parents of Supreme Athlete Mentoring Program, I adore you guys. You guys entrusted me with your children and that means the world to me. In a time where trust is very tough to come by, you guys have consistently allowed me to provide guidance and nurturance to your child. Ultimately you believed in my vision, and for that I 'am humbled and honored.

- To the countless volunteers and support staff at Supreme Athlete training session, thank you guys so much. I would not be able to do some of the awesome things in the community without you guys. Special shot-out to my man Gabe and "Big Lo". Coach Lo you are truly a life saver man. You have been consistent and never left me hanging alone to build the young people and help them reach their dreams. Thank you so much champ. I couldn't do this without you brother.

- To Hartford, Connecticut you have provided countless memories and experiences which has allowed me the courage and insight to write this book. I' am thankful to the city. The good, bad, and ugly. I hope this book can inspires someone from the city to rise above whatever conditions and reach back in help others do the same.

- To all the athletes out there with a dream of playing D1 sports, never let anyone tell you what you can't do. If someone else accomplished this goal, you can too! I encourage you to study your field, and master your craft. Make this goal a part of your lifestyle. Each and every day you should be doing something that will help you further your positon toward achieving this goal.

- To my beloved children, daddy loves you dearly. You guys may not fully understand the process daddy has to go through to make a better life for you guys, but know this, your lifestyle will be of luxury and high class. You guys will enjoy the fruits of mommy and daddy's labor. I promise to introduce you guys to hard work and appreciation. Our family legacy will be founded upon service, gratitude, and an abundance of health and wealth. Oh, and you guys will be in my next book on how I prepared my children to become D1 athletes. Lastly, Sy you are nothing short of amazing girl. You are literally the reason I' am able to share these experience with the world. You are the reason I have been able to be a blessing to so many families through sports mentoring. Thank you so much for being my friend, and life partner. I love you girl, keep shinning, and being a blessing to so many people in the world. I couldn't have chosen a better mother for our children.

Pre-Game

One of the great gifts of mentoring is that it's never one way. Because I've mentored some of the greatest young athletes in the country, I've been able to perfect the formula that I first began developing, although without realizing it, as a young athlete learning the game.

Before I take you down this amazing journey of youth sports and scholarship attainment, I want to take a moment and tell you how this book is written and who it is written for. My writing style mimics my persona in being diverse. I employ multiple styles to fit the specific subject matter. Similar to an ordinary conversation where you may have someone using comfortable speech, but if the topic is more scientific they try to honor the field by using a more technical or research style jargon. In this book you will be exposed to a technical style, research style, and conversational writing style. I believe this will not only keep you stimulated, but also be authentic to my personality. There will be moments in this book where it may seem like I'm sitting next to you having a discussion, and in other sections it may seem more like a school setting where I 'am informing you as a teacher would in the classroom. Regardless of the writing style, I want to be clear on who this book was written for. *I wrote this book for you--the parent wondering how to raise a young athlete and what steps to take to earn a D1 scholarship, the student-athlete preparing to compete for a college scholarship, and the coach/trainer who wants to better navigate the college recruiting scene.* I'll be transparent in saying that this book was not written to generate extra income. Humbly speaking, I' am very blessed in the area of finances. This book is meant to add as much value as possible to those who play a role in helping young athletes earn D1 scholarships. Hope you enjoy.

If someone like me had been around in the early days of Stanley "Stack" Williams's athletic career, my chances of going Division I (D1) through the front door instead of the back would have vastly improved. Once I crossed that threshold, though, I paid close attention and took careful notes on the valuable lessons offered by elite sports, in general, and by the game of football. Today, as an athletic consultant, I help young athletes avoid many of the pitfalls I encountered. I guide them through the highly competitive web of elite sports. The road to D1 sports, scholarships, and careers can be rocky even for the most talented athletes.

The gap in the marketplace of expertise in cultivating D1 athletes inspired me to create the position of Sports Mentor & Consultant (SMC), which I currently hold as the founder and CEO of the Supreme Athlete Mentoring Program, a nonprofit based in Connecticut where I grew up.

Over the last five years, I've developed a plethora of D1 athletes. Their successes in school, sports, and the community have proved repeatedly my longstanding belief that mentoring makes a huge difference in the options that open to young athletes. As an SMC I provide the following services:

- Utilize a holistic approach in guiding youth athletes ages eight to eighteen.
- Advocate and create timelines for athletic development and experience.

- Facilitate contact between college recruiters and private prep or public school coaches.

- Make referrals to specific athletic camps conducive to the athlete's long-term goals.

- Develop and implement marketing, personal branding, community outreach, and manage charitable sponsorship and media relations.

- Manage the progression of the athlete until his or her goals are met.

I'd like to tell you a little bit about myself before I earned the college degrees and became a CEO of a non-profit agency.

Growing up in Hartford, Connecticut, I was a multi-sport athlete. My background is like many African American men from inner cities across the country. I never knew my father. He was murdered when my mother was six months pregnant with me. Although she worked hard, life was a struggle, and she relied on public assistance to take care of me. We lived in neighborhoods that exposed me to unimaginable violence and the ruthless behavior that claimed my father's life. As a child, I witnessed shootings and killings. At one point, like many of my peers, I got involved in gang activity. It was a matter of survival. Being raised in a single mother household didn't seem like much of a struggle back then, but knowing what I know now, I can imagine how difficult it was for my mother. This also helps me realize how strong she was as a teen parent. My mother had such a sense of urgency in the way she raised me. I'm not sure where she got it from, I'd like to believe it derived from the everyday struggle of her peers, and our overall environment. She knew I had to 'be a man' someday so she was driven to make sure I was a great man. The lessons my mother taught me as a child were invaluable. Here's an example of some of the lessons. Between the age of 7 and 10 years old we had to carry our dirty clothes in trash bags to the laundry mat which was about one and a half miles away. Those bags were so heavy, but my mother did not have a vehicle nor did she have an excuse on why she couldn't get the job done. That was a lesson on hard work and having no excuses toward completing the objective. Daily chores were mandatory. My mother would curse me out for the smallest things like moving her pillow case from one section of the couch to the next without placing them back where she had them. She taught me as early as 5 years old how to cook, fight, iron clothes, separate dirty clothes to wash, unlock and lock the door with my own set of keys, and to never talk to strangers. My mother never really sat me down in a traditional sense and taught me anything, she kind of just made me do things that were conducive to being a responsible person, regardless of my age. The one thing my mother would emphasize to me on why she was teaching me how to be domestic in the home was that she didn't want me to rely on a woman to do those things. Being on welfare also provided many life lessons growing up. Sometimes we would take public transportation to the welfare building to process paperwork which basically was to justify why we needed assistance from the government. Even this episode in my life was a phenomenal lesson in which my mother taught me about preparation and organization. Those visits to the welfare building meant that my mother would have to prepare a ton of documents for the caseworker to evaluate and she also had to keep them organized or we would be in jeopardy of losing our government benefits. Safe to say that never happened. Currently, people joke about how organized I 'am to be a 'man' in comparison to most men in the world. I must credit my mother for that. These lessons have carried over to my adulthood very well. Once I became old enough to play sports, my life would change drastically. There wasn't a stable male figure in my life as my mom would date different guys, but no one really stood the test of time nor played a significant role in my development. The one person she dated that did have somewhat of an influence on me was in-and-out of prison, so that didn't last long. So sports took on the role of father figure in the sense of positive male coaches being consistent and reliable in my life. These men would further the lessons my mother had instilled in me, but from a male perspective. The reason I decided to provide a little more depth about my mother's parenting style is because there is a large percentage of mothers' with athletic children, in particular young men, who I believe may benefit from an aspect of my childhood. I had an amazing relationship with my mother. I believe her style in raising me was suited for the times and necessary for me to become a responsible man someday.

The way sports saved my life is by instilling life lessons, an appreciation for rules and a sense of community and belonging. I was introduced to organized football around 1994. Before then, I played *Rumble Fumble*—one player versus everyone else to score touchdowns—with my friends in the neighborhood. But I never developed a real understanding of the sport. As far as I was concerned, football was just a bunch of hard-core rough stuff. This street version of the game made me feel strong and tough. So, hey, I was down with it. At school, we played on the concrete because there were no grassy areas or fields for us to play. Looking back on those conditions, I understand why old schoolers think the younger generation is soft. Our environment was rough, but my classmates and I truly enjoyed the game. We were too busy having fun together to notice our disadvantages. Plus, we equated tough times as part of our rite of passage into manhood.

One day, this guy, who eventually became my first head coach, handed my friends and me a permission slip to play football for a local youth football team called the Vikings. By this time, I'd started to earn a reputation for my tackling abilities. I brought that paper home and handed it to my mother, a young parent who knew nothing about sports. She was just happy if I kept busy and safe while I was out of the house. Parents at that time did not allow children to sit around playing video games all day. There weren't any iPads, iPods, iPhones, or any damn thing else with an "I" in it. We truly used our imaginations, or we played outside all day until the streetlights came on at night. Sometimes our parents even let us play under the light when it got dark.

Day one of practice was out of this world. Nothing prepared me for the level of running, screaming, and more running and screaming that I endured. Our sole activity involved running and getting yelled at to the point I wondered if we would ever actually touch a football. I later learned that what we went through was "conditioning." When we finally started handling a football, it was even worse. We ran the same play over and over. At eight and nine years old, I started to get bored and wanted nothing to do with the sport, at least from an organized standpoint. A week went by. I found myself still running, getting yelled at, and running the same play over and over. But on this day, we were issued equipment, and things took yet another turn for the worse. We did an exercise called "The Oklahoma Drill".

We were partnered with a teammate to go up against two other teammates. One partner's job was to block a designated partner from the opposing side while the other one was to run toward the end zone in the direction instructed by the coach. The idea was for the player to develop the skills, confidence, and creativity to find his own way to the end zone.

"Seeeeeeeeeet Hut-Hut."

My skinny little nine-year-old ass took off only to be met by this 5-foot 9-inch Hispanic kid, named Alexis. Built like an ox, Alexis looked like a grown ass man. He drilled his shoulder pads into my stomach, simultaneously wrapping his arms around my legs, lifting me off the ground and slamming me like a slab of meat onto the ground. The wind was completely knocked out of me. All I could hear were screams and grunts from my teammates and coaches. When I finally caught my breath, I cried my eyes out. I learned two important lessons in that moment of vulnerability: (1)

This was my initiation into football, and (2) I was not ready.

I wanted to run home and cry to my *mommy*, but I knew that would not sit well with her. I kept it a secret. I kept going to practice. I was officially a football player. Despite my rough start, overall my first year was successful. My team won the city championship. And I got used to the yelling, running, and practicing the same play over and over. By this time, my reputation for bone-crushing tackles grew and my nickname "Stackem-up" or Stack, for short, stuck.

As the years went by, I added basketball, boxing, and track to my activity list. I was interested in all three sports, but I did not have as much time as I would have liked for boxing and track. Basketball and football became my favorite and foundational sports. I played basketball the most, followed by football. My personality was influenced by these sports. Basketball appeared to be associated more with a pretty-boy persona compared to football, which was perceived as more ferocious and no-nonsense. I thought it would be cool to have a balanced personality, so I played both sports for as long as I could.

In 1998, I entered high school. The high school I attended had a reputation for being the worst academically in the state. It was alleged to have high rates of HIV and sexually transmitted diseases among the student population. I witnessed robberies, sexual activities, and anything else that you can possibly imagine in the hallways. The environment was horrible, to say the least. But, believe it or not, the one bright spot at this school was its athletic programs. It offered the three most important sports to a youth from the inner city: basketball, football, and track. My high school excelled in these sports. Between the three, we won state titles each year. During this phase of my life, I became aware of a shift in my view of the world. I realized I stood in between two worlds: one of poverty and one of potential.

The poverty I lived in was a cyclical reality for most African American youth from the inner city. I was born into this condition, but I saw a potential outlet through sports, if I chose to pursue it. Sports opened a window into a world of opportunities beyond my neighborhood. By the time I was a high school senior in 2002, I had garnered a ton of trophies and accolades from playing sports. I also established lifelong bonds.

My grades during my first two years of high school weren't great. I was a decent student by my junior year and became an excellent student by my senior year. What happened? Typical story here: I started to realize that the University of Florida was not flying a recruiter to Connecticut to visit me and offer a scholarship if my grades were not excellent. I was a bit too late for that one. I received a bathtub's worth of college interest letters (which mean little, and I will explain later), but I was not eligible based on my grades and SAT scores. This forced me to attend a small college in West Virginia for one semester, and then I went off to a junior college/community college (JuCo) with a football team. Once I landed there, I was able to start over and focus on earning a Division I (D1) scholarship and going to the NFL. I dreamt of purchasing my mother and grandmother a house and retiring them from work.

JuCo is not for the weak minded. It was an eye-opening experience for me. For the first time in my life I was classmates with kids from all over the country. They were from the West Coast, South, Midwest, and East Coast. The mixing of all these personalities and cultures was a recipe for disaster at times and other times a tasteful blend of different cuisines. Fights, arguments, scandal, betrayal—you name it and it happened on that small college campus in Upstate New York. I won't reveal the name of the college, but it was truly an experience. Had I not been raised in a tough environment, I would not have survived. My football experience and perspective changed drastically as I had to raise my standards when it came to training, studying film, and competing. I had never played against kids from different time zones who *expected* to play in the NFL because many people from their hometowns did it.

Here is a quick example of how I was forced to change my mentality about the game of football. I was in my dorm room after an exhausting day of practice, and I overheard my teammates who lived next door to me, who just so happened to be from Florida say, "Aye dawg, we gotta sho dees up norf folks how we get down in da souf. Dees boys don't kno-bout no football maaan. Dey basketball players up here. We do dis dawg."

As he was saying this in his southern dialect, they were getting dressed to go to the weight room for another session. I thought to myself, "What the hell are they doing? They are crazy. We just finished a dreadful practice, and now they are about to go train some more. Yikes!" I realized I needed to reevaluate my approach to the game if I wanted to buy my mom and grandmother a new house someday. So as the season went on, this experience inspired me as I began noticing how willing I was in making *sacrifices* to succeed. I noticed how those kids from Florida weren't the only group of kids working so hard. When I walked downstairs to other floors in my dorm, I heard similar discussions among the other players from places like Virginia, California, and New Jersey. Players expressed a sense of *expectation* when they spoke. They had experienced so much *exposure* to what D1 talent looked like that they seemed unbothered by *sacrificing* so much to reach the D1 level.

Meanwhile, I was coming from a place that, from an athletic standpoint, historically could not match up with where these guys came from. I had to make a decision and make it quickly if I wanted to reach my goal of playing D1 football and going to the NFL. I immersed myself into the Florida boys' culture of high expectations and willingness to sacrifice. I placed myself around these kids from the 305 and 954 area codes. It was like everything I had learned and understood as hard work and work ethic were false.

These kids embraced me and truly taught me how to work on my craft and dedicate myself to my athletic goals. Outside of practice, the competition between the players from different parts of the country was intense. Being *exposed* to these battles influenced how I expressed my athletic prowess. Having *access* to these things helped me see what areas I needed to improve if I was going to continue playing this game that I was introduced to in 1994.

During my tenure at JuCo, I earned high interest from Clemson, Oregon State, and Syracuse University. I still had the University of Connecticut (UCONN) as an option, which I eventually pursued because I wanted to live near my child. Yes, by this time I was a teen parent. My daughter was born the year I went away to JuCo. I was only eighteen. I wanted to pursue my football dreams, and I wanted to be near my child and be a part of her life.

My experience at UCONN was an eye-opener on so many levels. I had to "walk-on" the team, so the lens I saw things from was a little different. Fortunately, for me, I was pretty talented (and I'm not just saying this because I'm writing this book). I made the team with flying colors because I understood those lessons taught to me by my Florida boys while at JuCo.

A walk-on is a player who was not awarded a full-aid scholarship to enroll at the school. I had to walk-on the team due to changes in the coaching staff. The guy who recruited me had taken another job. Therefore, their preferred interest in me was gone. A walk-on must take advantage of the government-funded Free Application for Student Federal Aid (FASFA) program and academic

scholarships.

Walk-ons are treated a little differently when it comes to

certain opportunities and benefits. Depending on your actual talent

level and "swag," or persona, it doesn't matter if you're a walk-on.

If you're just one of those players who's a hard worker, but not

talented enough, then you will most likely be treated like a second-

class player and not enjoy some of the fruits of being a D1 athlete.

The contrast between the benefits of playing at the different levels

came into focus for me. In high school, and even JuCo, we had

some of the worst condition equipment and had to pay for

everything we wore. At the D1 level, everything was free and

abundant, and to be honest this also including sexual experiences.

Before I move on, let me be clear about the previous statement on

everything being free and abundant including sex. I realize the

unfortunate climate of rape going on across the country on many

campuses so I want to be sensitive to that. But what I'm saying

here is that as a male D1 athlete, I had consensual privileges with

females that the average student on campus did not have. I'm not sure of the exact reasons, but if I had to guess, it could be due to the popularity and notoriety of being a D1 athlete. Not to mention the potential of becoming a professional athlete might have crossed some of the females mind.

At each level of football from 1994 to 2004, as the competition increased, the number of kids willing to commit and sacrifice decreased. According to the National Collegiate Athletic Association (NCAA), 6.8 percent of athletes play football after high school, and only 2.6 percent play at the D1 level. Those who make it to D1 earned it. I will delve deeper into the reasons later in this book.

My running back coach told me years later, after I graduated, that I was a victim of timing. What he meant was, had I enrolled two years earlier than before I did, I would have been in the discussion for first string. That's D1 for you, though. Timing is key because you can be the star in one season, and then some kid from Los Angeles (or any major city for that matter) can commit to the team and outshine you during spring ball or summer camp and your stardom is finished. I quickly learned the meaning behind a word that I had heard often in my hometown in Connecticut: *politics*. People used this word to describe why they didn't succeed at something. A former All-State player who went off to college and had an unsuccessful career would blame politics. I never understood what that really meant until I got a firsthand view of it while playing D1 football.

Politics meant if you didn't know who you needed to know, weren't connected to whom you should have been connected to, or simply did not establish a great enough relationship with a decision maker, you were *assed out*. At the same time, an element of accountability must be factored into the equation when it comes to a successful versus an unsuccessful sports career. Many athletes tend to blame politics as an excuse for their own shortcomings. They simply can't fathom that they did not put in the work or fell short of expectations from their coaches. Either way, it is their fault that they did not flourish at the collegiate level. Ownership of their role in the situation hasn't settled in yet.

D1 provided me with a wealth of memories. I was able to fly across the country to compete on nationally televised games. I stayed at some of the finest hotels and ate as much as I wanted of the best-quality food. I met amazing people from different parts of the country and played with and against guys who would eventually play in the NFL. I was featured on a PlayStation videos game three times. And most important, I accomplished my goal of playing D1 while earning multiple academic degrees.

I want to reiterate, I wrote this book for the parent, student-athlete, and coach/trainer as you all play a vital role in the attainment of a D1 scholarship. Now grab your highlighter so you can mark key points as I delve deeper into my formula of '*Going D1*'.

Stanley "Stack" Williams, SMC
Founder and CEO
Supreme Athlete Mentoring Program

2006 Media day in college.

1st Quarter

Expectation and the Cultural Effect

The prospect must be groomed by people who expect the athlete to be the best in the country

What is "expectation"? According to an online Oxford dictionary: *A strong belief that something will happen or be the case in the future . . . A belief that someone will or should achieve something; students had high expectations for their future*

Expectation is closely related to the word *confidence*, which means "full trust; belief in the powers, trustworthiness, or reliability of a person or thing: We have every confidence in their ability to succeed . . . Belief in oneself and one's powers or abilities; self-confidence; self-reliance; assurance." Now, let's look at the word *culture*.

According to Dictionary.com, *culture* means:

"Development or improvement of the mind by education or training . . . the behaviors and belief characteristic of a particular social, ethnic, or age group: Anthropology. The sum of ways of living built up by a group of human beings and transmitted from one generation to another."

When individuals set their standards or expectations higher than the norm for themselves, it increases their chances of accomplishing the expected outcome. I'm not talking about magical thinking here. Expectancy must be backed by a strong work ethic and focus. When talking about athletics, many variables are involved. But high expectations lay the foundation. And a culture of excellence must be established within the environment, if an athlete is to be successful.

Culture is passed from generation to generation through language as well as through modeling behavior. In this process, important, desirable, or undesirable traits and behaviors are defined. Within a culture are norms and behavioral expectations. These cultural norms dictate which personality traits are valued. In the early 2000s De La Salle High School, a high school in

Concord, California, was on a 100-game winning streak. I could

not figure out how in the hell were they consistently beating

everyone. They were blowing out teams. The culture and

personality of that team was to habitually dominate. Younger

athletes from that community saw and heard about that

powerhouse team's performance. Naturally, they wanted to be a

part of that. So, winning became the "norm" for the next dozen

years.

Considering cultural influences on personality is important

because Western ideas and theories are not necessarily applicable

to other cultures (Benet-Martinez & Oishi, 2008). There is a great

deal of evidence that the strength of personality traits varies across

cultures. This is especially true when individualist cultures, such as

European, North American, and Australian, are compared with

collectivist cultures, such as Asian, African, and South American.

People who live in individualist cultures tend to believe that

independence, competition, and personal achievement are

important. In contrast, people who live in collectivist cultures tend to value social harmony, respectfulness, and group needs over individual needs. These values influence personalities in different, but substantial, ways. For example, Yang (2006) found that people in individualist cultures displayed more personally oriented personality traits, whereas people in collectivist cultures displayed more socially oriented personality traits.

In a May 21, 2015, *Forbes* (forbes.com) opinion piece, Leigh Steinberg, a contributing writer, explored the unique cultural attributes of a pioneering group of coaches from islands in the Pacific, including Polynesia, Hawaii, and Samoa, and the athletes they produced. They came from cultures that valued family and the work ethic. One coach acknowledged feeling a sense of warmth and spirituality among the Samoan athletes.

He said, "There is pride instead of jealousy for the accomplishments of other athletes. Passion for every activity is bred into young Samoans." Five years earlier, Scott Pelley drew attention to this cultural phenomenon in a report on *60 Minutes*, stating that a child with Samoan parents was 56 times more likely to make it in the NFL than any other kid in America.

A March 2003 online article in the *Journal of Sports Science and Medicine*, underscoring the important role cultural factors play in athletic development, is relevant today. It spotlighted Canada as an obvious example of the role culture plays in the environmental equation. Hockey, which has a longstanding and deeply entrenched history there, is an integral part of the country's national identity. Many of Canada's national heroes, past and present, are ice hockey players.

Canada's "northern climate and numerous lakes and rivers provide opportunity to play outdoors for considerable portions of the year, and public money has been used to build a large network of ice hockey arenas throughout the country," the article noted. The country also boasts an extensive club system that encourages children to start playing the game at very young ages. Given these cultural and environmental factors, it is no surprise, then, that Canada is known internationally for its success and for the stars it produces in the sport. Similar factors pertaining to Alpine and cross-country skiing can be found in Austria and Nordic countries, respectively.

The combination of natural landscape, public enthusiasm for skiing, and the adoration heaped on ski heroes is a potent incentive for developing expertise in the sport. The belief that people from certain countries possess genetics that make them especially suited for sports has yet to be supported by science. Yet, amazingly, the search for genetic explanations immediately becomes the focus when a group dominates a sport. The dominance of Black athletes in basketball is a prime example in American sports.

More recently, Kenyans' dominance in running events has renewed discussions around genetic advantages. But as many experts point out, the preoccupation with genetics overlooks much more compelling cultural and psychological influences. This holds up in America, where once racial barriers were removed, Black athletes have come to dominate certain sports. Basketball, football, and track and field, sports they tend to excel in, are generally supported in the public-school systems they attend.

The country and private club settings where sports such as golf and tennis are taught have a long, well-documented history of discrimination against Black and other non-White groups. Even as the policies of denying membership to Black and other groups have changed, these exclusive settings still present class and social barriers.

Environmental factors and expectations influence the culture within a team itself. When you look at the NBA during the Detroit Pistons' Bad Boys era or the NFL's Oakland Raiders during the 1980s, you can see they built a culture of high level aggression and intimidation. Or, in modern times in the NFL, you have the New England Patriots who have built a culture of winning, plain and simple. The same goes for NCAA football and the University of Alabama or NCAA men's basketball Duke and UCONN women's basketball. Internationally, Usain Bolt, the legendary sprinter from Jamaica, has managed to make everyone believe that the island of Jamaica has the fastest humans on the planet. It's cultural.

Culture and expectation have played a major key in players earning scholarships. According to the NCAA in a report posited by www.sbnation.com, in 2015-16, Football Bowl Subdivision (FBS) and Football Championship Subdivision (FCS) teams recruited about one in ten Floridian high school players. The Sunshine State is way ahead of everybody else, with Georgia (8.6 percent), Louisiana (8.1 percent), and Washington, D.C. (7.2 percent), all close. Seventy percent of the country's four- and five-star recruits over the past five years have been clustered in 10 states. Texas, Florida, and California produce more of those star recruits than any other states by a wide margin, with Georgia next. Per capita in the total population, D.C. has the most four- and five-star recruits. But that's misleading, since D.C.'s just one small city. Louisiana, with 1.58 blue-chip recruits per 100,000 residents over the past five years, stacks up best in that metric.

What the NCAA is counting here is more specific: college recruits out of a total pool of high school players. Florida's dominance in this stat has something to do with geography. Florida has 11 Division I programs (7 in FBS, 4 in FCS), tied with Louisiana, New York, Pennsylvania, and California for the third most of any state. Texas has 20 D1 programs, way more than anybody else, and North Carolina's second with 14. Texas is four times as big as Florida by land area, and California's more than twice as big.

It's a lot easier for the teams in Florida to move around and recruit prospects. Pennsylvania and New York's D1 teams are mostly FCS, with smaller recruiting operations. The same is true, to a lesser extent, of Louisiana and North Carolina. Florida is the most ideal state to get the most players possible recruited. If you're a high school football player with D1 dreams, there's no better place to live than Florida. If you have ever wondered where the most dominant athletes come from, you're not alone. I have, too. Areavibes.com, an online portal that tracks and analyzes sports data from around the country, suggests measurably high levels of expectations exist for certain sports in different regions. A review of the trends within three major sports reveals that the power of expectation and cultural effect varies from city to city.

According to Areavibes.com, across all possible cities in the three major professional sports, Chicago has had the most baseball (370), basketball (125), and football (464) players born within its city limits. Another city that produces a significant amount of talent, and placed second behind Chicago in football (231) and basketball (103) and fifth (231) in baseball, is Los Angeles, California.

Where did these players get the confidence and know-how to be amazing athletes? Again, it's really no surprise here. They are from environments with an intense sense of urgency and high expectations among athletes. Not expecting to "go pro" or D1 would be out of the ordinary. There is a large percentage of young people across the country who enthusiastically say they would like to be professional athletes when they grow older. However, most of them will not accomplish this goal. A determining factor is the cultural expectations within their immediate environments. If they don't have reference points, including image associations, then their environment lacks factors critical to their success. For example, a young man or woman who comes from the same community as Hall of Famers and MVPs is more likely to believe supreme achievements are expected of them. Or, as the adage goes, "Birds of a feather flock together."

In 2017, I participated in a seminar on how to attract wealth through learning financial principles. The place was packed with wealthy people who were in tax brackets far above mine. But I knew there was a benefit to be gained just being surrounded by a culture of wealth building. I kept an open mind. The facilitator was a millionaire investor by the name of Tim Payne. I jotted as many notes as I could because I knew that the principles and examples he laid out could be applied not only to my individual financial planning but also to programming D1 athletes for success. Tim emphasized three important points: (1) eighty percent of wealth has to do with programming, (2) being broke is a habit, and (3) exposure is the equalizer for wealth.

Athletic superiority starts with your immediate culture. One's culture must align with the aspired direction to increase the probability of reaching the goal. A culture of D1 expectations, followed by a culture of work ethic, is essential if you want to increase your chances of becoming a D1 athlete. To date, my nonprofit mentoring program "Supreme Athlete Mentoring Program"

(SAMP) has an 85% success rate of helping student-athletes earn

full scholarships to private prep schools and/or D1 universities.

How are we doing this? Well, the culture established and

maintained here is one of National focus. Basically, our athletes

understand that enrolling into our program requires a complete

mental transformation. A transformation that includes absolute

focus in acquiring specific knowledge and skill-sets. The level of

mental intensity and physical stress will cause a sane normal

person to quit or take a different route toward accomplishing their

dreams of playing D1 sports. There have been some student-athlete

who enrolled and quit our program, some have tried to do their

own thing and ended up at a lower level college (D2-D3) or quit

playing sports altogether. I truly believe life revolves around

energy. The energy that we invest in a particular thing will be the

energy returned in that area. But when you mix ego and pride into

a matter, you can almost bet you will end up on the losing end of

the equation. It is not a matter of discrimination, it is simply

energy. Those student-athletes who thought leaving our program

would be the answer to their D1 dreams lacked true understanding of the power of culture. Our culture was founded on national relevance and earning D1 scholarships. Our entire focus was dedicated to increasing the chances of accomplishing this, so in hindsight it made no sense to leave a culture like ours and either create one with no reference point on how to do so, or be led by someone who has never been to the destination before. Always remember this law: The prospect must be groomed by people who expect the athlete to be the best in the country.

Coach's Corner

When I entered high school in 1998 in Hartford, Connecticut, a small high school in a neighboring suburb produced a lot of D1 football athletes. The school won numerous state titles and was even mentioned on a national level by *USA Today* because of their controversial winning-point margins in games. The town was Bloomfield, home to the Bloomfield War Hawks, coached by Jack Cochran. During his coaching tenure, Cochran's teams beat other teams so badly that the governing body of high school sports in Connecticut put a ban on beating a team by a certain point margin. It was called the Cochran Rule. Cochran became legendary for sending so many players to D1 colleges. Out of those D1 players, a few even went on to play in the NFL, Canadian Football League (CFL), and Arena Football League (AFL). The real story behind this legend comes from the players. One former player said that Coach Cochran made the weakest player on the team feel like the strongest, and players literally were willing to run through a brick wall for him. Another player stated that Coach Cochran created a culture with a relentless work ethic and an attitude about winning that made it seem like the only option. Cochran went on to coach at other high schools. He won multiple state titles at each school, and he continued sending kids to D1 programs. Oh, by the way, his son also went D1 as well. His name is Casey Cochran and he played for UCONN before enduring a career ending injury.

2nd Quarter

Access and the Psychological Effect

The prospect must have access to other elite players, coaches, or facilities on a consistent basis

What is Access?

According to Dictionary.com, it is:

The right or privilege to approach, reach, enter, or make use of something.
A way or means of approach or entry.
The opportunity or right to see or approach someone.

Without a doubt, having access to supreme or elite people, places, and things can have a positive effect on an aspiring D1 athlete. The best of things in life are usually protected or kept in a category called exclusivity. Terms such as *VIP*, *first class*, or *members only* are examples of this. When athletes are growing up playing sports, they are presented with this fact in many scenarios. One of those scenarios is in youth sports clubs, such as the Amateur Athletic Union (AAU) basketball. In AAU basketball, if a team is not sponsored by brands like Nike, Adidas, or Under Armour, then the athlete must pay to join that organization. This is where things get tricky.

Many youngsters from the inner city cannot afford to pay up to $1,500 for tournaments and training. A couple of their peers from the suburbs on the team technically are off-setting the cost for some of the inner-city players. This is one of the ways that the system is structured. The suburban parents understand its value to them. It gives their youngsters access, too. Traditionally, in sports such as football, basketball, and track and field youth from urban communities outperform their peers from the suburban communities. Access to playing with these supreme athletes on a consistent basis can have a positive psychological effect on the youth from the suburbs. It helps their development process.

Exposure to great athletes enables them to assimilate their winning habits and traits. Access to elite players is a great way to motivate untapped talent within an individual. Many coaches use this strategy to improve the ability of weaker players in hopes that proximity to better players will drive them to work harder at elevating their level of play.

There are no guarantees here, but it can have a positive effect on self-reflection for the weaker players who aspire to improve their game. Being surrounded by people considered elite creates a psychological effect for the individual. This effect can be crucial in efforts to boost an athlete's confidence. During my high school years, we had a philosophy about our basketball team. We said our worst player was better than most schools' best players. Basically, we had an amazing squad. I believe we could have been separated into three teams and each team would have made it to the state championship. We were that good because we had access to one another. When an entire team is good, all players positively affect one another, even the so-called worst players.

This also applies to access to elite coaches and facilities. Coaches who have a history of developing D1 athletes tend to have a formula that works. These types of coaches develop an eye for identifying ability before it is actualized. Elite coaches know how to get the best out of their players, and they are aware of the necessary steps. Coaches with this type of wisdom are invaluable for an aspiring D1 athlete.

As a youth, I vividly remember a coach who was considered the best little league football coach in the city. This guy went to the championship every year, and everyone could predict it. I had to play for this team. I begged my mother to sign me up to play for him and what do you think happened? I was playing alongside other elite players from across the city, and we were playing for this elite coach who had the formula to develop talent and be successful as evidenced by making it to the championship each year. This coach had already established a foundation for his organization, and that was "winning." The coach made sure we knew from day one that we did not lose a game, and it started in practice. We competed against one another as if we weren't teammates. It was brutal. But I sincerely believe this is why we won all of our games and played in the championship. We eventually lost that game to our crosstown rivals, but most of the players on my team went on to high school and had successful careers and even played college football.

Sports science and medicine research has begun to reveal that athletes who have access to an expert coach have notable advantages, including the benefit of access to someone who knows how to create an optimal learning environment. Coaching experts are precise in their planning and goal setting than their non-expert counterparts. Legendary UCLA basketball coach John Wooden is an often-cited example of the time and meticulous planning and attention to detail that an expert coach puts into preparing each practice for players. All his players were constantly engaged, whether it was in a drill or shooting free throws during a practice.

In a study of coaching expertise in volleyball, Cobley (2001) found that athletes were active in drills more than 92 percent of the scheduled practice time, and the intensity level was equivalent to that faced in matches. Like Wooden's approach to coaching basketball players, it was found that expert coaches in volleyball knew how to structure optimal practice environments, which recreated the conditions of actual games, including the pressure.

In addition to a coach's ability to maximize practice time, the expert coach also possesses domain-specific knowledge that is essential to fostering improvement, particularly as the athlete advances in skill level. Rutt-Leas and Chi's (1993) examination of novice and expert swimming coaches supported these assertions. The coaches observed underwater video recordings of four swimmers of different skill levels and were then asked to analyze the strokes and to provide instruction. While novice coaches offered a somewhat superficial analysis using vague descriptions, expert coaches were very precise in their assessment and specific in their recommendations for improvement. Expert coaches had the ability to extract more from the information presented and could provide fundamentally better solutions to perceived problems. Rutt-Leas and Chi (1993) concluded that the expert coach displayed the same kind of domain-specific expertise that has been documented in other fields.

An important question to consider is at what age should athletes seek out expert coaching? Early studies focusing on the specific requirements of working with younger and less technically proficient athletes (e.g., Bloom, 1985; Smith et al., 1979) proposed that in the early stages of development athletes require primarily technical instruction to develop proper fundamentals, along with a high degree of support and praise to encourage continuing participation in the sport. They described an important part of the coach's role in the early years as being kind, cheerful, and caring. Only when athletes were older and more highly skilled would a coach require sophisticated knowledge and advanced qualifications.

Recent work by Côté and Hay (2002) supported these assertions and suggested that, while advanced coaching qualifications were deemed necessary in the later stages of development, coaches working with children at the initial involvement stage needed enthusiasm and facilitation skills above and beyond any technical expertise in the sport. Clearly, both the practice structure and the domain-specific knowledge of coaches are highly relevant to the progression and development of athletes in sports.

Facilities play a significant factor in developing a D1 athlete. Access to elite facilities creates a mentality that one deserves and belongs to top-notch infrastructure, equipment, and instruction. This feeling of belonging supports the psyche in boosting self-esteem. Confidence increases the chance of success in any field. Like Coach Calipari of the University of Kentucky men's basketball team, "I've always believed talent attracts talent". This philosophy helped calm his apprehensions when he lost his initial recruiting class of John Wall, DeMarcus Cousins, Eric Bledsoe, and Daniel Orton after his first season at the school. After he reached the Final Four the following season in 2011 with a brand-new core of players, he said in a *College Hoops Today* report with Jon Rothstein of *CBS Sports*, he could put together eight straight super classes based on that philosophy.

"They want to be coached. They want to be taught,"
Calipari said. "They want to be with other really talented people."

Because he's signed 31 five star athletes during his time at
Kentucky, it's a common misconception that he signs any and
every prospect with the capability of being a one and done.
Calipari will be the first to tell you this isn't so. In the interview
with Rothstein, he said athletes who are into drinking, smoking,
clubbing, and chasing women shouldn't even bother coming to his
program.

Moreover, Calipari is specific about the mentality he looks
for in athletes. One of the indicators he looks for is the mind-set of
an athlete as he sizes himself up against his prospective teammates.
Players who look in the gym and think they're the most-talented
ones in the gym are in the wrong place, he says. But, "If you look
in the gym and look around and go 'Wow, the talent in this gym,'
you're in the right place. Players come to Kentucky to get better,
he told CBS. "We undersell and over-deliver. This isn't for
everybody."

Calipari clearly understands his brand. He has done an exceptional job of creating a culture of excellence and, ultimately, pathways to the pros. Calipari surrounds his players with the best players in the world each year, and this type of access to elite players creates not only a sense of belonging and worthiness but also expectations for continued growth and elevation in talent development. I believe the weakest player on Calipari's team could transfer to another college and do well, simply because of the psychological effect of having access to what elitism looks like at the University of Kentucky.

Consistency is essential in these type of environments. Having access to other elite players, coaches, or facilities on a regular basis increases the chances of becoming a D1 player. As I stated earlier, nothing is guaranteed, but this will certainly improve the likelihood of it happening. They say it takes 21 days to make or break a habit. So, can you imagine the effectiveness of years of consistent access to an elite environment on an athlete?

Look at the airline seating categories in 'coach' versus 'first-class'. First-class is typically more expensive and offers more amenities compared to coach. First class passengers will most likely have stronger financial backgrounds and social networks. Access to first class can benefit any passenger. It opens a new level of networking opportunities during the flight. Useful business ideas and information may likely be discussed. This is not to say quality interactions do not occur in coach, and there is always the chance no one says a word to anyone in either seating arrangement. However, all things being equal, the probability that one will benefit more from the first-class seating arrangement is increased because the environment is more impressive, including in the minds of passengers flying first class.

Consistent access to any environment is a strong determining factor in an individual's mentality and experiences in life. Extreme examples of this, such as the way a criminal thinks, and the mentality of the world's wealthiest 1 percent, have long been the focus of social science research. It has been found that abusive people who engage in criminal behavior often were the victims of abuse themselves. It's cyclical. They had consistent access to people who engage in the same type of behaviors.

Although it's a different kind of access, the same principle holds true when you look at wealthy people. This access represents habits of financial freedom. There is a constant reminder of ways to sustain the status quo of that wealth. And whether someone is born into this culture or is placed in it, consistent access to it will improve the probability of an individual experiencing tremendous success.

Habits and discipline displayed by wealthy groups across the world are what separate them from the rest of the 99 percent. In these types of families, every detail is important to maintain the wealth status, even when it comes to marriage. Wealthy families are more inclined to ensure marriage happens between other wealthy families to keep the status quo alive and flourishing.

Many D1 athletes follow in the footsteps of their parents who had professional careers in their sport. I'm sure some may say they were born with an athletic gene. Now, I am not denying the possibility of this. Some offspring excel, and sometimes they even exceed their parents' achievement. Being born to a sports superstar imposes unique pressures and burdens. Growing up under the shadow of a father's greatness sets an unusually, if not

an impossibly, high bar. But I also know there are some athletes

who are born to professional athletes who do not play or ever

perform to the level of their parents. Unfortunately, whichever

sport they chose to play, their heritage automatically sets the

expectation regardless of the level of their athletic abilities. Having

a former pro athlete for a parent does not ensure failure. But

experience has shown that the extraordinary amount of pressure

alone is enough to derail even the most promising prospects'

development early on. Here are some high-profile examples from

thesportster.com of athletes who were unable to reach the heights

their parents reached.

- In a career that lasted 21 years, Cal Ripken Jr. is regarded as one of the best players in the history of baseball. His father was a renowned coach for the Baltimore Orioles. Cal was a star on the field and separated himself from his old man and created his own definitive legacy. Now, his son Ryan looks to do the same. Last year, he was taken by the Washington Nationals in the 15th round. Prior to that he was a 20th-round pick by the Orioles in 2012. He's yet to crack the pros and while he could live up to the high expectations that surround him as he matures, he just isn't anywhere near his father right now.

- Jerry Rice was known for his intense work ethic, great hands, and big play ability. He is hands down the greatest receiver to ever play in the NFL. But his son Jerry Rice Jr. is still struggling to make an NFL roster after going undrafted last year. Rice Jr. signed with the Redskins after trying out with the Ravens and 49ers. Considered a long shot to make the team, he was waived shortly after. Still a free agent, he might not get another opportunity in a league that's full of capable and talented pass catchers.

- With a player as talented as Michael Jordan, it'd be strange for him to have not passed any of his on-the-court skill to his children. But we'll never really know for sure if he did. Marcus Jordan isn't an example of someone who couldn't succeed but rather someone who was busy living off his father's name. He was unable to handle himself as a young athlete should. Of the many public mistakes he's made—including being arrested in a parking lot, costing his school an Adidas deal, and he and his brother blowing $50,000 of their father's money in Vegas—Jordan proved that his mind-set wasn't focused on basketball but instead on living off his name. He never even finished his collegiate career, and we'll never know how good he could've been because of a plethora of stupid, immature decisions.

There are many more cases in which children outperform their parents, such as Kobe Bryant and his father, Joe "Jellybean" Bryant. Here is a list of other parent and child duos.

Notable NFL father and son duos:

Clay Matthews Sr. and Clay Matthews Jr.

Howie Long and his son Chris Long

Oliver Luck and his son Andrew Luck

Archie and his sons Peyton and Eli Manning

Other notable NBA father and son duos:

Bill Walton and his son Luke

Tim Hardaway Sr. and Tim Hardaway Jr.

Mike Dunleavy Sr. and Mike Dunleavy Jr.

Doc Rivers and Austin Rivers

Gerald Wilkins and Damien Wilkins

Rick Barry and his sons Brent, Jon, and Drew Berry

I strongly encourage parents with athletic children to put

forth their best effort with ensuring their children have some type

of access to the lifestyle they would like them to experience. If

you physically cannot provide the desired environment for your

child, then you should find someone who can. Do not feel inferior

or insecure because someone else may be able to provide what

your child requires. It takes great strength to recognize this

inability and take the proper steps to identify who can. Taking this

approach has the potential to literally change the course of your life for generations if done correctly. In my field of profession, I've provided full access to my resources and networks for my athletes. Parents who were unable to provide such resources invested in my services and it has yielded multiple D1 scholarships. Each scholarship estimated to worth over a half million dollars in sports experiences during the course of four-five years in college. These parents often send me text messages pouring their hearts out and sometimes even crying tears of joy because of the working relationship between myself and their athletic child.

Some examples that can be used to help provide access to elite experiences for an aspiring D1 athlete to follow:

- Watching YouTube videos of professional athletes or elite peers and mimic their training habits

- Befriending elite athletes over social media and inquiring about their daily routine

- Attending games or practices of the most successful teams/players in your area

- Talking to someone who's accomplished what you would like to accomplish

I currently mentor and train a young man who prior to coming to me had zero D1 football scholarships, he now has a total of 19 and counting within a matter of two years. He enrolled in our program as an 8th grader. He is now a sophomore in high school. I strategically aligned him with certain athletes to compete with and against on a consistent basis. I created his timeline of activities to participate in and through the support of his family, and his willingness to follow the D1 formula, he is rated top 3 nationally in his position. Always remember this law: The prospect must have access to other elite players, coaches, or facilities on a consistent basis.

"Success is not a random act. It arises out of a predictable and powerful set of circumstances and opportunities."—Malcolm Gladwell, *Outliers: The Story of Success*

Coaches Corner

The successful youth football team that I was a part of in

1997-1998 had an interesting twist for some of the players. There were two relevant high schools in the city, and my teammates and I would split up between the two schools. Half the team enrolled in each high school. This proved to be a fatal blow to the success of some of the players. I decided to attend the high school that had all the success in multiple sports. Although it was not an ideal intellectual environment for a child's growth, it was the best option available to grow from a sports standpoint. The other high school was mediocre in success and had been out of favor athletically a few years prior. My teammates who were very talented on our youth football team would end up being average athletes because of having access to a mediocre high school with mediocre players, and coaches.

Meanwhile, those of us enrolled in the more athletically successful high school grew exceptionally fast. My ability tripled that of my peers from youth football days. I was surrounded by guys who had just won multiple state championships, and the expectation was to continue winning more. These players and coaches created a culture of dominance in the game of football, track, and basketball, which positively affected my psyche. I was completely engulfed in this culture, and it proved to benefit my athletic experience.

Another example is a program out of Bradenton, Florida, called IMG Academy. I could write an entire book on them alone, but I will keep it brief here. This institution has positioned itself to be the best place in the world to be if you want to increase your chances of becoming a D1 player in any sport. IMG has world-class coaches, players, and facilities. They play a national schedule, which means they only play the best talent in the country. IMG's facilities are so good that NFL teams and players train there as well. I am personally inspired by this institution as they represent nothing but success for an athlete. Of course, there are many areas of growth and development for a human being. But my focus here is strictly from an athletic standpoint. From that perspective, they are positioning themselves to be the gods of high school sports development in America.

3rd Quarter

Exposure and the Physical Environment Effect

The prospect must display their abilities against other elite competition in front of real decision makers, such as college recruiters or talent ranking personnel.

Dictionary.com

Exposure:

1. The act of exposing, laying open, or uncovering:

2. The fact or state of being exposed:

3. Disclosure, as of something private or secret:

4. An act or instance of revealing or unmasking, as an impostor, crime, or fraud:

Exposure. Exposure. Exposure. I cannot stress this point enough. The athlete *must* be exposed to what a D1 athlete looks like to not only position himself or herself but also to understand where they are in their own ability. According to the definition, exposure is the act of uncovering or disclosing something private or secret. Elite players typically try to work-out with other elite players because they eventually realize that the importance of improving their craft will depend on who they spend the most time with.

Athletes who aspire to become D1 players must understand this concept. Exposing yourself to elite players consistently can create a psychological effect that manifests itself in work ethic and motivation. Let's take a step back for a moment. I want to start from the birth of a child to that child growing into a prospective D1 athlete. Studies have found starting children in an active lifestyle from infancy may not only improve their health but may also enhance their coordination and confidence and encourage a lifetime of fitness. Habits formed in childhood are often hard to break. Encouraging active play in babies and toddlers helps them to develop strong muscles, improve coordination, and boost confidence.

My children are an example. Currently, my two youngest children are five and three years old. My five-year-old intrinsically loves gymnastics and dance lessons more than any other activity, but she does not mind participating in basketball, soccer, or track. It's probably because she wants to make me happy. My three-year-old is a monster in all things physical. She intrinsically loves soccer, basketball, boxing, track, and anything physical. She and her sister are complete opposites. The oldest loves combing her dolls' hair and wearing her mother shoes and purses, while the youngest likes to jump off couches and throw items across the room. Both girls have something else that's very important to them and that's their love for me. This strikes up immediate competition. Neither one of them wants to look bad in front of dad so they are more willing to put forth extra effort in the areas they don't naturally perform well to get my attention.

I learned early how to positively manage their behaviors based on this assessment. I place them in environments where other kids are more advanced than they are. But with me being present at their practices, they must elevate their concentration because not only are they competing for my approval, but they can't let dad see them get outperformed by other children. This dynamic helps my children grow exceptionally quicker than other children because I study their learning styles intensely. The environment helps a great deal as well because the other children are advanced, and my children must focus more than they normally would, which causes immediate growth through consistent exposure.

Many experts believe it takes a minimum of 10 years and at least 10,000 hours of training for an athlete to reach elite levels. Known as the 10-year rule, the idea of this kind of exposure was popularized by Malcolm Gladwell in his book *Outliers*. However, the rule was first advanced by Herbert A. Simon (Nobel Prize, 1976) who was interested in the role of knowledge and expertise. The theory has been discussed over the years in publications such as the *Journal of Sports Science and Medicine.* And it has been supported in music (Ericsson et al., 1993; Hayes, 1981; Sosniaki, 1985), mathematics (Gustin, 1985) and, of course, athletics. The research suggests the training involved in attaining expertise is practice. The forms of training are not necessarily motivating and frequently require high levels of effort and concentration. They do not lead to immediate social or financial rewards.

A summary of the characteristics that distinguish the expert (Singer & Janelle, 1999) is worth reviewing here:

- Experts have greater task-specific knowledge.
- Experts interpret greater meaning from available information.
- Experts store and access information more effectively.
- Experts can better detect and recognize structured patterns of play.
- Experts use situational probability data better.
- Experts make rapid and more appropriate decisions.

Parental influence on exposure is essential for an aspiring D1 athlete. Parents must make calculated decisions regarding their child's athletic development and various investments, including emotional, physical, financial, and psychological. Research on the topic has appeared in sports journals. For example, a 30-year study examining three stages of talent development (Bloom et al., 1985)

affirmed what many parents of elite athletes learn from firsthand

experience. Demands on parents shift at each stage of the athlete's

development—the early, middle, and later years. Initially, parents

assume strong leadership roles, providing their children with the

opportunity to participate in a sport and maintaining direct

involvement in their practices and training. In this stage, the

emphasis is on fun and learning basic skills. As the young athlete

transitions to the middle years, parents' and athletes' commitment

increases. Parents invest more time and resources into their

children's sports activity and seek higher levels of instruction for

them. During the later years, parents continue to play a supportive

and nurturing role while their young athletes assume greater

control of planning their sport careers and future.

Each phase along the continuum of athletic development

presents increasing demands and pressures. Parental interest is

essential to providing the emotional and practical support elite

athletes need to overcome the challenges they encounter, such as

injuries, fatigue, and financial barriers to training. Athletes whose parents are unable to provide them access to elite exposure have difficulty gaining the high levels of practice they need to achieve expert performance.

In my experience with youth sports development, I have noticed a reoccurring fact: The athletes who are exposed to elite talent on a consistent basis tend to raise their level of expectations for themselves, and their output drastically changes. One factor that affects this is financial resources. I realized early on in my career that I was at a disadvantage economically. Everyone in my community was poor, which forced us to become extremely resourceful. We put items laying around to good use and took advantage of plenty of free park space. Out of boredom, we created athletic games. A few games to note:

Knock Knock, Zoom Zoom: This was a game of risk that reinforced acceleration skills. The objective was to knock on a stranger's door inside an apartment or a residential area and when you heard them coming, you ran as fast as you could away from that door. If you got caught, you would have to deal with the consequences of playing on people's property. Very risky behavior.

Catch Me, Kill Me: This game was a test of speed. The objective was to not get caught by opposing team members. After teams were selected, you would run for your life and hide until someone caught you and beat the hell out of you with their teammates. That was enough motivation to make sure that you didn't get caught, which increased your speed for sure.

Red Light, Green Light: This universally known game helped with reaction speed. One player turned his back to us and closed his eyes while yelling out one of three traffic light colors. The other players acted like cars and had to obey the traffic light colors. This game helped with acceleration and reaction time because if you get caught by the person yelling out the colors, you had to return to the starting line.

Tag: This game was similar to Catch Me, Kill Me; however, a safe place, or base, protected you from being tagged "it." The person that was "it" had to chase and tag someone else, who would then become the chaser. As you can imagine, endurance and agility were the focus.

These games are a great way for children who come from economically disadvantaged backgrounds to develop athletic skills. But what about other areas of life? Does this same notion apply? I decided to think of other areas of human activity in which I could test my theory. I reflected on romantic relationships and how they develop and strengthen.

I mentor an athlete who is from Africa and attends a predominately white private prep school. He is a very talented football player, an All-American with more than 20 D1 scholarship offers. This young man is 6-foot-1 and weighs 230 pounds of pure muscle. He possesses a charming personality and great smile. Attending this private school affords the young man different luxuries. He is surrounded by some of the most affluent families in the country. He has access to many different opportunities, and the academic expectations are much higher in this elite environment.

A statement he made to me as we drove home from

practice one day revealed an area that may cause him some problems later in his life. I asked him what are his thought on race relations in America as it relates to dating. He said, "I mostly date white girls. Black girls have attitude problems and too much drama. Plus, I am surrounded by mostly white girls anyway."

This young man's opinion reflects a reality shared by many young superstar African American athletes who attend affluent schools where the majority of students come from wealthy backgrounds. In this setting, they are exposed to elitism in most areas of student life. While there is nothing wrong with dating who you are attracted to, there is something wrong when exposure is limited to one ethnicity. That's a topic for another book. My point here is that my mentee's exposure to only affluent Caucasian girls has instilled in him a narrow perspective of the world. At the same time, this exposure has afforded him opportunities that many young people of his ethnicity rarely gain access to.

Another young man that I mentor, who is also African American and a D1 football prospect withvC.lk more than 20 scholarship offers, has a completely different viewpoint based on his daily exposure. This young man attends a public school whose student population is more diverse than the previously mentioned private school. When asked his opinion on race and relationships, the athlete from the public school said, "I date whoever looks good to me. I really don't have a preference right now. It doesn't matter to me. But I've probably dated more biracial girls than any other type."

This young man's choices appear to be based on his exposure to people from a broad range of ethnic backgrounds. He is more open than the other young man, who preferred Caucasian women, to the idea of dating young women from diverse ethnic backgrounds. Neither athlete is wrong in their dating preference. My point here is that their level of exposure influenced their feelings on race based relationships.

Let's review another example—crime. When children are consistently exposed to violence and criminal behavior, this builds a sense of normalcy and a mentality of criminality. Even if these children do not exhibit criminal behavior, they still may be affected. Studies show that children who grow up in communities with high unemployment rates are more likely to be

exposed to criminal activity. Even if the reasons given for the crime are survival, such as robbing or selling drugs to meet basic needs such as food and shelter, these are clearly wrong choices with negative consequences. But from the perspective of exposure, youngsters growing up in these circumstances often find it hard to see other options. Those who can make good decisions and hold themselves accountable deserve acknowledgment. However, sadly, their numbers do not match the overwhelming percentage of those who succumb to the negativity and exposure to poor examples of life management.

There is a saying I like to tell the young athletes that I mentor, "If you hang around five losers, you'll turn into the sixth one." Phrases like these come a dime a dozen. In fact, here are a few more that speak to some of the things that I refer to in this quarter:

- *Monkey see, monkey do*—Following an example because you're consistently exposed to it.

- *Birds of a feather, flock together*—People who are into the same types of activities tend to spend a lot of time together.

- *The apple doesn't fall that far from the tree*—Referring to a child of a parent who displays similar if not the same attributes of the parent.

Exposing an aspiring D1 athlete to actual D1 athletes and other aspiring D1 athletes is a necessary step toward making the dream a reality. It's like a cheat sheet. When you place a young athlete in this environment, you increase that young athlete's chances of earning a D1 scholarship. This strategy is what I call the *preferred cyclical effect*. When it comes to maximizing exposure, a new aspect that's been added to the high school recruiting game is the ranking system. These ranking systems are created to differentiate talent levels—a tool college recruiters can use if they desire. These online platforms dedicate countless hours of reviewing and researching film on athletes to determine who's the "duds" from the "studs" region to region. Some sites are more legitimate than others, so do your homework to determine which are credible. Here's an example of how ranking systems work:

Ranking personnel, who work for a network that focuses on high school basketball or football recruiting, attend a free regional camp for high school athletes. Ranking personnel then observe the athlete compete and perform physical tasks associated with that sport. The ranking personnel identify a couple of studs, take note of their jersey numbers, and find his or her way to that athlete. They converse; social media information and phone numbers are exchanged. The athlete is now on the radar because of their performance.

The athlete attends and dominates a few more similar camps and earns "stars." One to five stars can be earned, with five being the best of the best. The more stars an athlete earns, the higher the ranking. This system has caused some controversy because some athletes feel it is unfair, while others love it because it separates them from the rest of their peers. These stars have the capacity to increase an athlete's scholarship earning potential. However, the star system does not guarantee that any scholarships will come the athlete's way. It all depends on the coaching staff philosophy on recruiting.

Now that the athlete is on the radar, if that athlete is from a little-known school in a small town, the chances of recruitment increase because college coaches see the news about the athlete on social media platforms on a consistent basis. At this point, the athlete starts to receive random messages from coaches, inviting the athlete to attend their university camp to display his abilities in front of the coaching staff. The staff can then evaluate the athlete using their measuring tools. There are a few smaller steps in this scenario, but this is the gist of how it goes.

One of the most important elements of this entire process is about the *real* decision makers. Perhaps you've heard this story before. A young athlete becomes a local basketball star at the community YMCA, Boys and Girls Club, or recreation center. This athlete gets all the attention and continues doing well against his local peers, and everyone expects this kid to become a big-time D1 athlete. Everyone tells him how great he is and local coaches invite him to join their teams for bragging rights in the community. He gets older and his career isn't guided by someone who's played or coached at the collegiate level and understands the proper steps.

The kid doesn't play for a nationally sponsored AAU club to broaden his exposure, nor does he have access to train with or against other elite athletes. He's a senior in high school and has zero offers. Small schools from the local area are the only colleges showing interest. What happened here? The answer can be found in the first, second, and third quarters of this book. The kid had expectations from his peers, but these expectations were empty because he was not exposed to other athletes who performed the tasks expected of him. Therefore, he didn't have a reference point.

He also didn't have access to other elite players, as he was the main attraction in his area. There were no other kids to compete or train with. He was not exposed to talent from across the country through an elite AAU basketball club. He spent too much time earning local bragging rights on local teams that played in community tournaments. When this young athlete was razzling and dazzling the local community, no real decision makers were around. There was no one who could say, "Okay, this kid is the real deal, and I must introduce him to someone who knows the formula of helping athletes earn scholarships to the D1 level."

There were no recruiters or coaches anywhere near the performances of this athlete. It's not about what you do as an athlete; it's about who sees you do it. There have been performances that were nothing short of magnificent, but they were showcased in front of inconsequential bystanders.

Let's take football, for example. There are high school players who are praised locally but have yet to make their mark on the national scene. Therefore, they can only attract local attention and praise. The athlete may have some skills but compared to athletes across the country, they are a joke! Athletes in this situation probably are aware of their shortcomings, but their pride and ego refuse to allow them to be embarrassed. Either way, they do not reach their full potential because they refuse to challenge themselves. This type of athlete may run a 40-yard dash in front of his friends or high school teammates in excellent time, but the problem is no real decision maker was present. Once again, the people who saw his performance are insignificant to making the D1 dream a reality. As young athletes understand the importance of doing the right things in front of the right people, their athletic experiences change drastically.

A couple years ago on a Saturday afternoon a father approached me at one of the biggest basketball tournaments in New England called, "Hoop Hall Classic." This tournament is reserved for the top high school basketball teams and players in the nation. I was fortunate enough to have met multiple current NBA players who were participants in this tournament. These type of events excite me because I understand the value of environments like this. Anyway, this father was introduced to me through a mutual friend of ours as he needed help supporting his son's football career. He showed me his son's highlight footage from his phone enthusiastically as he raved about his son's ability. I viewed it with apprehension because I know how parents can be swayed a bit by the athlete being their child. As I watched it, I had on my "evaluation eye" opposed to viewing it for entertaining purposes. I take this type of stuff very serious, so I wanted to be as transparent as possible with the gentlemen. After we spoke a bit about the highlight footage and his son's ability, we set a schedule to proceed with me guiding his son's career and helping his dreams of becoming a D1 football player turn into reality. In short, here is how I planned it out for this young athlete. The kid was a good player in a bad market, and he was raw in skill specific ability. But what he had was a relentless effort and fearlessness toward the game of football. So in essence, he was halfway there, he just needed some fine tuning and proper placement. I immediately assigned him to attend specific national combines, and university camps. Next, I made it a point for him to transfer schools to a more competitive program and one that meets his academic needs. The school he transferred to would compete against other D1 prospects who were just as talented if not better than he was. The parents were 100 percent on board and provided no resistance which I genuinely appreciated because sometimes fathers in particular can be a hindrance to their son's athletic career due to ego. Fast forward to the present year of 2018, this young man is rated top 25 in the nation in his positon and has over 19 D1 scholarships from some of the best programs in the nation including Ohio State, Penn St., Clemson, and Michigan.

Always remember this law: The prospect must display their

abilities against other elite competition in front of real decision makers, such as college recruiters or talent ranking personnel.

Coaches Corner

There was this kid I grew up with who could do things with a football that most people could only dream of. This guy was a pure athlete and could play almost every sport with minimum effort. We called him "Rocket". Rocket was a classic example of what should never happen to a student-athlete. Rocket's talent level was comparable to the kids who make it D1 and excel. This kid had it all. Rocket's family was solid from what I could tell, and he received a lot of love from them. I was never under the impression that he was lacking in that area. The areas in which Rocket suffered were exposure and expectations. Rocket grew up in the same area as I did, but he went to a high school that, prior to him, had not sent many athletes to D1 schools. No one on his team had the same or better abilities than he did. Rocket was a little league superstar, and he transferred his skill set to the high school level and became an All-Stater. But he never really made the transition to college the way his talent should have nor did he have anyone to nurture or cultivate his abilities. Rocket should have been playing in the NFL on Sundays.

Rocket was a great kid and rarely ever got upset or made anyone angry with him. He was just an overall nice guy. Presently (2018), Rocket still plays in local flag and semi-professional leagues where he continues to destroy defenders when he has the ball in his hands. The guy is thirty something years old, and it's like he doesn't age because he still causes headaches on the field.

Another local legend was "Beast," a basketball player. Beast's family dynamics were a little different from Rocket's. Beast seemed to come from deeper poverty. We all lived in the same community and witnessed similar atrocities in our upbringing. Beast was an absolute terror on the basketball court all through little league, AAU, and high school basketball. Beast's abilities were so amazing that he had to play with older kids to get a challenge. Even the older kids had serious trouble defeating

Beast on the court. Beast's academic struggles were his demise.
He could never really perform to the same level in the classroom as
he did on the court. Beast also should have been playing for a D1
program as opposed to attending multiple junior colleges before
eventually coming home and bouncing from one semi-professional
league to the next.

Beast and Rocket were similar in their personalities. They
both were great guys and did an excellent job staying away from
criminal behaviors in a crime-filled environment. Beast's issue
was not *exposure*, as he played for a nationally ranked AAU club
and did exceptionally well there. The areas in which he suffered
were academics and cultural expectations. From my understanding
he did not come from a family of athletes. Therefore, no one ever
played for a D1 program or even went to college. Rocket's issues
were exposure and cultural expectations. Rocket never trained
with or against other elite athletes, nor did he play against elite
talent. When Rocket played against elite teams during the high
school season, he did not perform as well as he should have
because he was not challenged day in and day out at his own

school by his teammates. Rocket was also a victim of proximity.

There were not many athletes in his immediate area on his level

nor were any former D1 players or coaches available to properly

guide him on his athletic journey.

4th Quarter

Sacrifice and the Personal Effect

The prospect must be willing to lose sleep, friends, or perceived moments of fun to become a D1 athlete

What is sacrifice?

According to Merriam-Webster.com:

Something offered in sacrifice; destruction or surrender of something for the sake of something else; something given up or lost; the sacrifices made by parents.

Let's look at this definition and use real-life examples to make sense of the explanation. The destruction or surrender of something for the sake of something else can be viewed in a few different ways. One example would be parents who quit smoking cigarettes to prevent their children's exposure to hazardous chemicals in their early development. For a student, forgoing a fun party with friends to study for a major test the next day would be an example of sacrifice. Throughout life, we are faced with challenges that could also be viewed as sacrifices. These decision points, I believe, are character builders. When we are in a position where sacrifices must be made, we should comply immediately. I was told that to whom much is given, much is required. The question becomes, what will an aspiring D1 athlete be willing to sacrifice to earn a full scholarship?

There are big and small sacrifices, but essentially it is all relative to the individual and their circumstances in life. One athlete could be from the inner city struggling against poverty, while another athlete may come from the suburban community struggling with entitlement issues or being ungrateful. Each prospective athlete has their own struggles. Each will be confronted with choices that call for making sacrifices toward the goal of earning a D1 scholarship. Some parents are willing to make tremendous sacrifices to support their children's athletic dreams.

Nick Heras and his parents were the subject of a 2011 CNN article titled "Going to Extreme Measures for Child Athletes" by Stephanie Chin. Their sacrifices offer insight into the lengths some parents are willing to go to support their children's athletic dreams. Nick Heras, 14 years old at the time and an aspiring quarterback, moved across the country to attend an elite athletic training program to the tune of more than $50,000 a year. Moving away from his family and friends was not an easy choice, but Nick said he knew that he had to attend the world-renowned IMG Academy program in Florida if he wanted to be serious about the sport. The program had a reputation for training children to become sports superstars. While his parents acknowledged that the financial sacrifice was substantial, they also noted the time and patience they poured into their son's football dreams in hopes that the payoff would come in the form of a full scholarship. A few years later, Nick would end up attending Trinity College, a D3 (Division III) Ivy League school. I know you're wondering why all of that sacrificing just to end up at a D3 school. I understand your line of thinking. There are no guarantees in anything in life, but you can improve your chances by putting yourself in positons to accomplish your goal.

The Herase's exemplify the extreme measures some parents are willing to take for the sake of earning a D1 scholarship. Not all families are able to make this type of sacrifice, which may seem unfair. However, life presents advantages and disadvantages regardless of which end of the economic spectrum an athlete's family falls. The Heras family took the steps that I would recommend for those that can afford it. For the family that cannot afford these measures, I would recommend that they identify elite programs, coaches, or athletes in their area and spend hours watching YouTube videos of professionals training or providing tips on mastering the craft in a sport.

I mentor a young man whose family has committed to driving him to my facility to work-out after he gets out of football practice at least three times a week with each ride being forty-five minutes to and from, totaling ninety minutes. This young man has developed much faster than his teammates physically and mentally by being in the environment that I talked about earlier in this book. The major key here is that he is training with other aspiring D1 athletes, and those who already have scholarships, which enable such a concentrated focus towards the goal. To date this athlete has earned over 21 major D1 scholarships to the likes of Florida, Ohio State, Michigan, Penn State, and many more: not only his sacrifices, but also his parent's willingness to sacrifice sleep, gas, and money all for the possibility of him earning a scholarship. As a consultant I often provide insight and resources for families whose children aspire to play college sports at the D1 level. I currently work with a family who travels from Connecticut to New Jersey two times a week for specialized skills and drills at the quarterback position. This same family has spent well over $5,000 each of the last three summers attending college camps all in the name of D1 scholarship attainment. In my experience, the most extreme measure displayed from a family that I work closely with has been done for a lacrosse scholarship. This young athlete is a Phenom at 12 years-old. His father has him on a work-out regiment in the morning before school, then he attends my personal work-out sessions after school, then he travels back and forth from Connecticut to NYC and Philadelphia on weekends. This family also incorporates rigorous academic programs for this athlete, which aids him in preparing for the workload that private school and college will present.

Again, these measures taken by this family may seem extreme to some, but to those who come from this type of culture, it's nothing short of common practice. I believe that families and athletes who put in the effort and sacrifice will experience the greatest gain. In the remarkable words of actor Will Smith, "Anytime you inject extremes into the universe, you can expect extremes to come back." Have you ever noticed how much weight you lose when you increase how often you run? Or when you run even when you don't feel like it during the worst weather conditions? How about when you incorporate waking up earlier than you're used to, which to some may represent extreme sleep sacrifice. People who sacrifice also display the level of selflessness that they have within themselves, especially parents who support their children's athletic development.

I'd like to focus on the newest family to receive tons of controversy and criticism because of a parent's brashness and big personality: The Ball family, headed by father Lavar Ball. The Ball family has three sons, Lonzo, LiAngelo, and LaMelo. Each child plays basketball at a high level. Recently, the oldest, Lonzo, was the number two draft pick in the NBA to the Los Angeles Lakers. His two younger brothers are All Americans, who verbally committed to UCLA on full athletic scholarships. Their father has stated that he started his three sons in sports as young as four years old with little league teams and training. He said he intensified their training as they got older. His sons sacrificed typical kid fun to develop their athletic talents. To some parents, this may sound like robbing children of their childhood. For others, like Lavar Ball and his wife, it is cultural. They both played college basketball and understood what it took to earn the right to play at that level. Lavar also played in the NFL briefly. These experiences enabled the Ball family to create a formula that improved their children's chances of playing at the highest level in sports. So far, this strategy has worked.

Many parents give up the time they would otherwise spend together as a couple. Dave and Kerry Clay from Michigan provide a further glimpse of the magnitude of the sacrifices that parents are willing to make. The couple has sacrificed time, money, and their personal needs so that their children could receive specialized athletic instruction.

"On weekends between October and March, Kerry and Dave rarely see each other, but they see a combined 100 hockey games," according to a story by Kelly Hill posted MLive.com. Further illustrating the depth of parental commitment to their young athletes, the same story reported that even during an economic downturn business at the community's gyms and athletic facilities did not drop off. During a six-month period, three new local gyms opened in Grand Rapid, and they reported either stable or increasing levels of business.

"It doesn't matter how tough things are, parents make sacrifices for their kids," said Stacey Ballinger, co-owner and head coach at Radiant Sportz. "Typically, parents will sacrifice for their kids first. Parents will do whatever it takes to help their kids be successful." Gyms usually offer programs for recreational gymnasts, cheerleaders, and USA Gymnastics competitive teams. While the cost of a recreational program can be as low as $15 per week, the cost of competitive team gymnastics can reach $300 per month in gym fees and another $300 per month in team fees per athlete, as well as travel expenses to meets throughout the Midwest and occasionally around the country.

Nathalie Hautala, a nurse at DeVos Children's Hospital, and her husband, Jim Hautala, who was unemployed for a year, estimated that her family paid more than $8,000 per year, plus travel expenses, for their gymnast and three hockey players.

"I sacrifice a lot," Nathalie Hautala said. "We don't take vacations. When we travel for hockey or gymnastics, that's our vacation. "It's hard to justify when you're behind on your mortgage and you still pay the gym, but this is what my kids love to do. When you see them out there doing what they love, you realize that the sacrifices are worth it."

Throughout my travels and research as a sports mentor and consultant, I have heard every side of the discussion. I do understand that youth sports can take a lot out of parents because of the high costs and demands on time and emotional energy. However, the rewards from youth sports outweigh the punishments. A 2012 *True Sport Report*, put out by the U.S. Anti-Doping Agency, cites a long list of advantages for playing sports. Here are a few from the 106-page report:

- Better classroom performance
- Greater personal confidence and self-esteem
- Stronger peer relationships
- More likely to make friends, including those of different races
- Greater connections with school—that is, greater attachment and support from
- Girls and young women engaged in sports are less likely to be overweight or obese, depressed, smoke, use illicit drugs, or have unwanted teen pregnancies

- Better able to acquire emotional control, learn the value of teamwork, and exhibit initiative

- Women who played sports in high school were 73 percent more likely to earn a college degree within six years of graduating high school than those who did not play (based on a 2007 study)

- Greater involvement in volunteer work

Some sports require more time, while others demand more money. The level of sacrifice varies, depending on the specific sport. Growing up in a poor community, my family did not have the financial resources to support my dream, so I participated in every free sport the city offered youth. Constant practice enables some degree of improvement. When the right genetics are added to the mix, things can pick up for you. An example of this was the athletic shift and transformation that occurred when I put down the basketball and picked up the football. As I grew, it became evident that my body type and personality were better suited for football.

I loved playing basketball. Knowing what I do now, it was

because basketball was more accessible. Historically, it's been a dominant sport in the Northeast. Football culture, on the other hand, is stronger in the South and on the West Coast, which is among the reasons many D1 football athletes come from these regions.

Few occupations or hobbies in the world require more sacrifice than sports. The amount of work required to be successful is on another level. It is daunting at worst and invigorating at best. Youth as young as five years old spend hours practicing and memorizing scripted plays to outsmart the opposing team. These measures are taken in the hopes of increasing the chances of not only earning a scholarship but also eventually playing professionally.

In a 2013 report on fox4.com, sportswriter Macradee Aegerter, examines the sacrifice of putting children through club sports through the lens of cost and benefit to the child. The answer ultimately depends on the goals of the young athlete. With only about 2 percent of high school athletes in the country being awarded athletic scholarships to compete in college, according to the NCAA, the competition is fierce. And it starts at the club level because most offers come from exposure to AAU tournaments, which is expensive. To a parent like Cynthia Perry, who put three children through club sports over the span of a decade and worked a second job to pay for it, the sacrifice has been worth it. She acknowledged the team work ethic and discipline that elite sports instilled in her children. But Perry also happens to be among the parents who have the satisfaction of realizing a concrete return on her investment.

After being seen by recruiters at AAU tournaments, her oldest son got a full ride to the University of San Diego for soccer. Her daughter played on a soccer and academic scholarship at Avila University. And her youngest son was on the radar for a number of D1 basketball programs.

"When they have free college later in life and some of those colleges were over 200,000 dollars, it's not a bad deal," Perry said.

Now, on the flip side of this equation, take a story like the late great Michael Jackson (MJ) and the sacrifices he made to become a world icon. Although he was not an athlete, the extreme measures taken for him to become a megastar illustrates the level of sacrificing some are willing to go through. The horrific stories of his upbringing have been the subject of documentaries, books, and news articles. Many attributed his childlike behaviors as an adult to the fact that he missed out on his childhood. Some might argue that the benefits of stardom outweighed the cost of his sacrifice and suffering. He amassed millions of dollars in his career, and he most certainly earned it as he became a master in his field. But at what cost? Again, I raise the question not to judge, but rather to highlight the level of sacrifice and dedication it took for him to master his craft and become a superstar.

Aspiring D1 athletes must understand the bigger picture and be willing to miss out on perceived moments of fun with their friends. This requirement is the toughest for teenagers. I find that teenagers have such a difficult time complying with sacrificing their friends or activities such as parties, trips to the mall, hanging out, or just sitting around on their phones and playing video games. The levels of distractions are much greater today than when I was growing up in the late 1990s and early 2000s. I find that most

student-athletes are unaware of their placement statistically to even

play at the D1 level. Here's some data to put things into

perspective:

NCAA RESEARCH
Estimated probability of competing in college athletics

Men

Men						
	High School Players	*NCAA Players*	*Overall % HS to NCAA*	*% HS to NCAA DI*	*% HS to NCAA DII*	*% HS to NCAA DIII*
Baseball	488,815	34,554	7.1%	2.1%	2.2%	2.8%
Basketball	546,428	18,684	3.4%	1.0%	1.0%	1.4%
Cross Country	257,691	14,412	5.6%	1.9%	1.4%	2.3%
Football	1,083,308	73,660	6.8%	2.6%	1.8%	2.4%
Golf	146,677	8,676	5.9%	2.0%	1.7%	2.2%
Ice Hockey	35,155	4,102	11.7%	4.6%	0.5%	6.5%
Lacrosse	109,522	13,446	12.3%	2.9%	2.3%	7.1%
Soccer	440,322	24,803	5.6%	1.3%	1.5%	2.8%
Swimming	133,470	9,455	7.1%	2.8%	1.1%	3.2%
Tennis	157,201	8,092	5.1%	1.7%	1.1%	2.4%
Track & Field	591,133	28,334	4.8%	1.9%	1.2%	1.7%

Volleyball	55,417	1,899	3.4%	0.7%	0.8%	1.9%
Water Polo	21,857	1,014	4.6%	2.6%	0.7%	1.3%
Wrestling	250,653	7,075	2.8%	1.0%	0.8%	1.0%

Women

Women						
	High School Players	*NCAA Players*	*Overall % HS to NCAA*	*% HS to NCAA DI*	*% HS to NCAA DII*	*% HS to NCAA DIII*
Basketball	429,380	16,593	3.9%	1.2%	1.1%	1.6%
Cross Country	222,516	15,958	7.2%	2.7%	1.8%	2.7%
Field Hockey	59,793	6,032	10.1%	3.0%	1.2%	5.8%
Golf	74,762	5,293	7.1%	2.9%	2.1%	2.1%
Ice Hockey	9,514	2,289	24.1%	9.0%	1.0%	14.0%
Lacrosse	88,050	11,375	12.9%	3.8%	2.6%	6.5%
Soccer	381,529	27,358	7.2%	2.4%	1.9%	2.9%
Softball	366,685	19,680	5.4%	1.6%	1.6%	2.1%

Swimming	166,747	12,356	7.4%	3.3%	1.1%	3.0%
Tennis	183,800	8,933	4.9%	1.6%	1.1%	2.2%
Track & Field	485,969	29,048	6.0%	2.7%	1.5%	1.8%
Volleyball	436,309	17,119	3.9%	1.2%	1.1%	1.6%
Water Polo	20,230	1,136	5.6%	3.3%	1.0%	1.3%

(http://www.ncaa.org/about/resources/research/estimated-probability-competing-college-athletics)

With percentages as low as some of these, aspiring D1 athletes must understand and be fully committed to the probability of sacrificial opportunities.

My mentality during my teenage years was awful. I remember it like it was yesterday. Here's an example of how I believed things were supposed to happen: I figured the older you got, the better you got, and naturally you would have to play in the NFL because your age required it. I never factored anything else into the equation. I was such a bozo during those years.

Although I was considered a top talent in Connecticut, I

was far from an elite athlete in the country. The top athletes during my time across the country were Reggie Bush, Vince Young, LeBron James, and Carmelo Anthony, to name a few. All these guys became professionals. Some of them will be in the Hall of Fame in their respective sports. As youth, they were consistently exposed to other elite athletes and made tremendous sacrifices to accomplish their goals.

In 2001, I read a notice in the local newspapers about a Nike football training camp being held at the Syracuse University. I asked my high school coach to take me to this camp so that I could measure my abilities against the so-called elite players on the East Coast. I was entering my senior year, and this was my first camp ever. By my current standards, as far as becoming a D1 athlete, I was already behind the ball on exposure. Arriving at the camp, I noticed how great it felt being among former All-American players from Syracuse and competing against some of the best athletes on the East Coast. I performed well enough in all my events that I was recognized as a top player in the region, which I thought was weird because I had never done any of the drills they asked me to do. To this day, I attribute my performance at that camp to playing multiple sports all my life and the immediate boost in my self-confidence from exposure to so much athletic history at Syracuse University. I never experienced that kind of confidence prior to being there. It was like I belonged among them.

There are circumstances in which young athletes are not fortunate to have any of the four elements described in this book; yet, they still earn D1 scholarships. They are often called *anomalies*. My response to this is, "Even a blind squirrel captures a nut sometimes."

Data supports the unfortunate likelihood that most young athletes will not make it to the D1 level to play sports. I have heard all the theories on why someone was unable to play D1 sports, and I've had enough. I want to help student-athletes, parents, trainers and high school coaches be informed on how to prepare an athlete to go D1.

I apply the four elements of expectations, access, exposure, and sacrifice with the athletes for whom I mentor and provide consultation. They have worked flawlessly thus far. I currently work with a young man who was told he was not a D1 athlete! I have been working with this young man since he was in the 7th grade (he's currently a re-classed junior) and he has always displayed exceptional athleticism. His high school coaching staff revealed these feelings to their peers in casual discussion and it got back to me through typical community gossip. To be fair, this young man work ethic was not the most impressive, where he shines bright is his athleticism and self-confidence. There isn't many athletes that I have come across that has been as confident as this kid. After ascertaining the young man's personal and athletic goals, it was obvious that his public high school was no longer the fit for him. I spoke to his parents and we put together a plan to elevate his status as an athlete and position him to accomplish his goals. Keep this in mind, at the time of that comment being made about not being a D1 athlete he had just finished his junior season, made All-State and had zero scholarship offers. I immediately increased my sense of urgency with him and we got to work. He requested to be transferred to a private prep school so he could re-class (repeat the same grade) and be surrounded by an environment that's conducive to his athletic goals. I helped him get a scholarship to the private prep school. When asked why he wanted to transfer, the young man stated, "I'm just not impressed with the past athletes scholarship offers here, nor does this program have anything else to offer me that I desire. I had fun, but I need to play with and against other aspiring D1 athletes who has bigger offers." Fast forward, the young man is now rated top 25 in the nation in his positon and has over 20 scholarship offers from the best universities including Michigan, Ohio State, Florida State, Penn State, Alabama, and many others. This comes with no surprise for me, but for the young man, he was a bit taken back when he realized how stressful this transition would be for him. Without going into too many details, the young man experienced some backlash from his peers and coaches who did not want him to transfer schools to pursuit his dreams. I don't believe they had malicious intent, but they were acting on their own personal goals for him and the overall team, which this kid was a star player on. The young man had to sacrifice a great deal to get arrive at this point. In fact, I would even allow him to stay with my family during the summer months to acclimate him to a D1 lifestyle with 5am morning work-outs. Always remember this law: The prospect must be willing to sacrifice sleep, friends, or perceived moments of fun to become a D1 athlete.

Coach's Corner

While playing D1 football at UCONN, I lost touch with so many friends at home. I was unable to maintain friendships due to the rigorous schedule we had to follow. At the D1 level, there is no such thing as a social life. Literally, we would wake up at 5 a.m., and our day would be consumed with football activities and school obligations until 11 p.m. That was it. So-called free time was devoted to either football or academics. The level of sacrifice that I had to endure during my tenure at UCONN was serious. There were times that I would meet up with a study group in the campus library, and we would study until 2 a.m. for our mid-term exams the next day. Mind you, I also had football work-outs in the morning at 6. Sleep was a luxury that I could not afford if I wanted to maintain my status as a student-athlete.

Athletes that were unable to meet the intense demands of the university or football team quickly found themselves with a minor consequence or, even worse, dismissed altogether. If you just *like* sports, then playing in college may not be the route for you. You must *love* playing sports because you'll be required to sacrifice so much time and energy from your life, that if you don't love it, you could literally lose your mind and suffer from depression. But, hey, like I tell the youth I mentor now: If you want to experience a $500,000 athletic journey in college (which includes apparel, food, travel, hotel, tuition, etc.), then you must be willing to give up something of that measure in other areas of your life, including sleep, friends, and whatever you may consider fun.

Overtime

Now, some of you may be wondering how to implement these strategies. I will provide an example for each step. Mind you, there are multiple ways to use the strategies in this book, but I will provide general ways to apply them.

1st Quarter: Expectation and the Cultural Effect
The prospect must be groomed by people who expect the athlete to be the best in the country.

Time, time, time. You must spend countless hours unlearning and relearning the athlete. This is a pivotal step because you must plant these expectancy seeds and water them constantly. Everything must be conducive to the athlete believing he or she can be the best in the country. You must use language, pictures, videos, and surround them with all the things that further the message. They say it takes 21 days to make or break a habit. I suggest you put this theory into practice. Also, you must make sure the people who spend the most time around the athlete have the same mind-set. We become who we spend the most time with, and our views on life can be affected greatly by our surroundings. So, please make sure the people who are in the aspiring D1 athlete's circle are on the same page. For my personal trainers and/or coaches out there, this also means not allowing your athlete to partake in local fun tournaments, or wasteful athletic events for the sake of the hosting group credibility. You must protect your athlete from any and all non-conducive experiences. By any means necessary!

2nd Quarter: Access and the Psychological Effect

The prospect must have access to other elite players, coaches, or facilities on a consistent basis.

Research! If you don't own your own facility like me, you *must* partner up with or find someone who does. I didn't always own a facility. I had to partner up with a local community center that had the tools I needed to help youth realize their dreams of becoming D1 athletes. If you're a parent, you may have to Google search gyms in your area and visit the site to see what type of people train there. If you're a coach, I suggest you collaborate with other high schools and put your best athletes with their best athletes in the off-season to train and compete regularly. Maybe even start a national 7v7 flag football league. It must be national to help with access to the best players across the country. This will only get them better, so please lose the egos! If you are a player, use your social media to inquire or locate a facility where the *big dawgs* go and join them immediately if you can afford it.

Sometimes, if you're a big *dawg* yourself, they will allow free access. The same goes for identifying an elite coach. I realize that some coaches are in denial about their status as some of them have had losing seasons for more than five years, but they still know everything. There are some amazing coaches out there. You just have to find them. Once you find an amazing coach, try to ascertain as much knowledge as you can from them. Most high school students must play for their district. However, if you get a chance to play for an elite coach outside your district, who has proven success by either their winning percentage or how often they send players to D1, then you should go for it. I've found that the private prep schools are more favorable for an aspiring D1 athlete. The prep schools have access to better classroom sizes, facilities, resources and overall support. Not to mention the competition level is usually greater due to the enrollment being open to students all across the world and allowing post-graduates to enroll. Don't get me wrong, there are some fantastic public high schools as well. You just have to identify what works for your goals.

You can determine the criteria, but if the goal is to play D1 sports, I advise you to find someone who has the strongest relationships with the D1 coaches. I suggest that the coach you identify is an aggressive hands-on coach who takes recruiting duties very serious and prepares his or her players to dominate the competition while in front of decision makers as often as possible. This coach must focus on recruiting year-round and not just after the last game of the season. It may seem like a lot for the coach, but the special ones know how to make it happen.

3rd Quarter: Exposure and the Physical Environment
The prospect must display their own abilities against other elite competition in front of real decision makers, such as recruiters or talent-ranking personnel.

Do not, I repeat, do not, allow the student-athlete to participate with other athletes who just play the game for fun and nothing else. This is a big no-no. Their lack of urgency toward mastery of the craft can negatively affect the athlete who aspires to play at the D1 level. The student-athlete must train with and play against elite athletes as often as possible or commit to their training regimen alone. It's better to train alone and focus on your craft than to be in the company of other athletes who do not share the same commitment level toward accomplishing the goal of earning a D1 scholarship.

Playing against the best athletes in front of the people who matter will greatly increase the probability of earning a D1 scholarship because these people have the juice, and they can make one phone call or text message that can change the athlete's life forever. I will caution you though, if you're a trainer or coach, or even a parent, most people who have mediocre goals and are primarily concerned with local achievements will not understand you. They may condemn you for not allowing your player, or child to be like the rest of the kids in the neighborhood. They need to maintain the status-quo to not feel left out. Well, I' am here to tell you, it's okay to go the other way. In fact, I encourage you to run down the road less traveled. Here is an example I like to share with the young track athletes I mentor. If you're winning your races at every meet, but you're competing against average runners, then it's safe to say you're the best of the worst runners. You see, it's not about winning the race per-se, it's about your time. Does your time meet or exceed national standard times in your respective events? That is the question you must ask yourself. Even if you are losing against the elite runners, there is still benefits to your performance. Your time is increasing because the amount of effort required to compete and potentially win is far more conducive to elevating your ability. If you play basketball and let's say you average 30 points per game. My question becomes, who are you scoring against? And who seen you score these points? These are key questions for any basketball player with intentions on playing D1 basketball. Now I know there are plenty of variables, including physical stature and position and things like that, but my focus is the environment in which the performance is taking place. This is why playing AAU basketball for nationally sponsored programs or competing in national tournaments is essential for aspiring D1 basketball players.

4th Quarter: Sacrifice and the Personal Effect
The prospect must be willing to lose sleep, friends, or perceived moments of fun to become a D1 Athlete

In his book *The One Minute Manager*, Ken Blanchard says, "There's a difference between interest and commitment. When you are interested in doing something, you do it only when it's convenient. When you are committed to something, you accept no excuses."

To determine whether your child or player is committed to becoming a D1 athlete, first you must make sure they know what it will take for them to play at the D1 level. This means you must not only explain but also show them visuals of other players participating at that level. You must also provide them with literature that details what D1 athletes go through to ensure they actually understand what they are trying to pursue.

If they agree to pursue this goal after these steps are taken, then the next step is implementation. I'd also like to add that aspiring D1 athletes must be willing to change their day-to-day schedules to resemble the schedule of an actual D1 athlete. This means, waking up at 5 a.m. and working out, watching film, eating properly, working out a second time during the day, and maintaining excellent grades, all at the same time. This process will require minimum time spent with friends or leisure time for your preferred hobbies alone.

The entire persona must undergo a transformation. This

transformation must be beneficial to accomplishing the goal of becoming a D1 athlete. Everyone involved in this process will also have to sacrifice at some level. The aspiring D1 athlete's coach may have to sacrifice time spent with family and leisure time with peers to focus more on helping the athlete attain the goal of becoming a D1 athlete. Parents will be required to invest more time and money in events and activities for the aspiring D1 athlete. Parents may have to either work longer hours or pick up another job to afford the equipment and specialized training that the athlete may need to position him or herself in a place where they can properly develop into a D1 athlete. In closing, read these words every day and I believe you will be closer to living your dreams:

"You are meant to have everything you love and desire. Your work is meant to be exciting, and you are meant to accomplish all the things you would love to accomplish. Your relationships with your family and friends are meant to be filled with happiness. You are meant to have all the Money you need to live a full, wonderful life. You are meant to be living your dreams – all of them! If you want to travel you are meant to travel. If you

would love to start a business, you are meant to be a business owner. If you would love to be a professional athlete, a lawyer, an inventor, an entertainer, a parent, or whatever it is you would love to be, you are meant to be it! When you wake up each day, you should be filled with excitement because you know the day is going to be full of great things. You are meant to be #1 in the Nation at whatever it is that you Love. You are meant to feel strong and safe. You are meant to feel good about yourself and know that you're invaluable. Of course there will be challenges in your life, and you are meant to have them too, because they help you grow, but you are meant to know how to overcome problems and challenges. You are meant to be victorious! You are meant to be happy! You are meant to be Supreme!" – Rhonda Byrne, The Secret – Laws of Attraction *(partially paraphrased)*

What are you waiting for? Get to work! Good luck, and I hope to read about your child or players sooner than later.........

About The Author

<u>Visionary</u>

Stanley "Stack" Williams, FOUNDER & CEO of Supreme Being Inc. has a vision of 'saving the world'. As cliché as it may sound, he is destined to accomplish this one way or another. Stack is a proud product of Hartford, CT where he attribute his balanced personality. Rooted deep from his grandparents, Stack was exposed to community service at an early age. He would soon be responsible for creating programs and initiatives through Supreme Being Inc. that positively impacts youth in diverse communities.

<u>Biography</u>

Stack's name emerged on the sports scene at the age of 9 where he would earn the name 'Stackem-up' from his bone crushing tackling abilities in youth football. As Stack progressed athletically, he became a local star and would eventually earn the rights to play Division 1 football at UCONN. Stack's dream of playing in the NFL would fall short although he was able to make it to the AFL's Georgia Force team before the league folded in 2008. Stack was determined to somehow stay involved in sports, so he volunteered with numerous youth sports teams and after school recreational clubs while completing his MBA program residing in Atlanta, GA.

Mentor

Upon Stack's return to his hometown of Hartford, he instantly immersed himself in youth sports and worked tirelessly to elevate the sports culture. Stack's first order of business was to create a program that catered to the needs of at-risk youth with supreme athletic abilities. Stack created 'Supreme Athlete Mentoring Program' which is offered under the Supreme Being Inc. umbrella.

Philanthropist

Stack also realized the importance of philanthropy so he organized annual initiatives that would spread awareness of social issues in the community. Some of these initiatives include:

- Back to School Book Bag Drive
- Local Small Business Career Fair
- Community Feast
- Self-Esteem focused Book Drive
- Financial Literacy focused Board Game Drive
- Clothing Drive
- Flag Football Scholarship Award Tournament

Stack's commitment toward improving the quality of life and inspiring young people in the community was also noted by other local community organizations as he has received multiple awards and key note speaker opportunities.

"We encourage our student athletes to be a part of the solution for their community. It is essential that our young people understand the importance of giving back and serving others. It is my objective to change the culture of athletes not giving back or coming back to where they came from to inspire others. Our youth continue to practice what we teach here at Supreme Athlete through our humanitarian initiatives." – Stack Williams

Athletic Consultant

Stack has added another role to his responsibility which is a 'Sports Mentor & Consultant'. As an SMC Stack is responsible for creating timelines for athletic development and facilitate contact with public/prep school and college recruiters. Stack also makes referrals to specific camps that are conducive to the individual long term goals. Stack conceptualize and execute marketing and personal brand strategies, community outreach, charitable tie-ins, and media relations. Overall, Stack holistically manages the progression of the athlete until goals are met.

Private/Prep School Scholarships

Through Stack's relationship building and networking ability, he has aided youth in earning full scholarships to attend private prep schools. Stack takes pride in being an advocate for youth who are committed to their dreams of playing sports at the highest collegiate level. When a child or family inquiries about prep school, Stack provides insight and guide them along the process. Stack's mission is to help youth reach their long term goal of earning a full athletic scholarship to college. From 2016-2018 Stack has amassed over $500k in private school scholarship fund for his mentees.

University Scholarships

The following universities are schools that have offered Full Scholarships to the youth that Stack mentors in Supreme Athlete. The training and mentoring that Stack provides throughout the year have benefited greatly as evidenced by all of these amazing schools offering a free education. From 2016-2018 Stack has amassed over $2 million dollars in college scholarship fund for his mentees.

- Univ. of Clemson
- Univ. of Alabama
- Florida State Univ.
- Univ. of Florida
- Virginia Tech
- Univ. of Wisconsin
- Univ. of Nebraska
- Univ. of Tennessee
- Univ. of Georgia
- Ohio State Univ.
- Univ. of Iowa
- UCONN
- Auburn University
- Univ. of Hampton
- Univ. of North Carolina
- Penn State Univ.
- Boston College
- Rutgers Univ.
- Florida Atlantic Univ.
- Univ. of Maryland
- Univ. of Kentucky
- Univ. of Duke

- Univ. of Hofstra
- American Univ.
- Univ. of Michigan
- Syracuse Univ.
- Univ. of Buffalo
- Temple Univ.
- Univ. of Texas A&M
- Univ. of Baylor
- Univ. of Rhode Island
- Univ. of Pittsburgh
- Central Connecticut State University
- Bryant University

Reference Page

1st Quarter:

- Google.com
- Dictionary.com
- https://www.forbes.com/sites/leighsteinberg/2015/05/21/how-can-tiny-samoa-dominate-the-nfl/#6ba5571ebfbb

- https://www.ncbi.nlm.nih.gov/pmc/articles/PMC3937568/

- https://www.sbnation.com/college-football-recruiting/2017/4/18/15340728/recruits-per-state-ncaa-map
- http://www.areavibes.com/library/hometown-heroes/

2nd quarter:

- Google.com
- Dictionary.com
- https://www.ncbi.nlm.nih.gov/pmc/articles/PMC3937568/

- http://kentucky.247sports.com/Bolt/Caliparis-discusses-Kentuckys-culture-recruiting-philosophy-48697532

- http://www.thesportster.com/entertainment/top-15-least-talented-children-of-legendary-athletes-2/

3rd quarter:

- Dictionary.com
- https://www.ncbi.nlm.nih.gov/pmc/articles/PMC3937568/

4th quarter:

- Merriam-Webster.com
- http://www.cnn.com/2011/LIVING/01/20/making.of.sports.superstar/index.html

- http://triblive.com/lifestyles/morelifestyles/7858866-74/says-sports-parents

- http://webcache.googleusercontent.com/search?q=cache:7erJFmCx4wUJ:www.mlive.com/articles/5043280/parents_say_personal_and_famil.amp&num=1&hl=en&gl=us&strip=0&vwsrc=0

- http://fox4kc.com/2013/07/09/more-parents-sacrificing-for-sports-but-is-it-worth-it/

Made in the USA
Middletown, DE
15 May 2018